100 australian poems for children

For Claude and Basil. CSM

For Bart, Harry and Pudding.
And in memory of Bruce. GR

Random House Australia Pty Ltd
Level 3, 100 Pacific Highway, North Sydney, NSW 2060
http://www.randomhouse.com.au

Sydney New York Toronto
London Auckland Johannesburg

First published in 2002, 2003 (twice), 2005, 2006, 2007
Text copyright © see acknowledgements
for individual poems
Illustrations © Gregory Rogers 2002

National Library of Australia
Cataloguing-in-Publication Data

100 Australian poems for children.

Includes index.
For children.
ISBN 978 1 74051 775 1.
ISBN 1 74051 775 X.

1. Children's poetry, Australian. I. Scott-Mitchell, Clare.
II. Rogers, Gregory, 1957 – . III. Griffith, Kathlyn.
IV. Title: One hundred Australian poems for children.

A821.00809282

Cover, text design and typesetting by Monkeyfish
Typeset in Savoy and Curlz
Illustrations created with pen and ink, ink wash
and Chinagraph pencil

Printed by Tien Wah Press (PTE) Limited, Singapore

Australia Council
for the Arts

This project has been assisted by
the Commonwealth Government through
the Australia Council, its arts funding and
advisory body.

100 australian poems for children

Edited by Clare Scott-Mitchell
& Kathlyn Griffith
Illustrated by Gregory Rogers

RANDOM HOUSE AUSTRALIA

Contents

Foreword

An anthology is like a pile of presents wrapped up and waiting to be opened. Some will be opened eagerly and then put down for later. Others might catch your eye and please you at once. Some you will want to share with others, while others you will want to keep to yourself. And there will be some (few we hope) that will be put aside to open at another time.

The poems in this collection make us think about what life in Australia is like: life before the Europeans; life in the early years of European settlement and what it is like to live here now. You will find poems written by children, adults, indiginous poets, recent settlers and even one by someone we have called an honorary Australian, Spike Milligan.

Many of the poems capture strong feelings, others tell a story or a joke, others leave us wondering.

Some poets have suggested the rhythms of galloping horses or the thudding of kangaroos. They have used long slow words to make us feel heat or the tiredness of old things, or short sharp words to describe the quick movement of a skateboard or the cold of frost.

What matters most in a collection of poems like this is that you will want to open this book over and over again. You might want to look more closely at those poems you weren't at first interested in — the unopened presents. You might want to re-read, or listen to, your favourites or look more closely at those poems that you don't fully understand. You might look closely at a line or an image that attracts or puzzles you and you might want to find other poems by poets you particularly liked.

We hope that this anthology will give you lots of pleasure and that it will encourage you to read poems in other collections. You might even want to start gathering poems for your own collection and perhaps start to write your own.

Clare Scott-Mitchell & Kathlyn Griffith

December

Elizabeth Honey

Purple carpet for the jacaranda.
Worn-out thongs on the back verandah.
Hot north wind. The smell of hay.
Coming for a swim today?

Skediddle, Skedaddle

Linda Stamatis

Skediddle, skedaddle,
My feet love to paddle
In rivers and beaches
And puddles and pools.

3

Bits of Me

Gordon Winch

I can slap
with my hand.
I can pat,
I can tip.

I can hop
with my leg.
I can run,
I can skip.

But what
can I do
with my chin
or my hip?

At least
with my lip
I can sip.

from
Fish Fingers
Max Fatchen

If you hold a shell to your ear, they say,
  You'll hear the sea winds blow.
I held one to my ear. It said:
  ''Ullo, 'ullo, 'ullo.'

I Live up There

Jane Bradley

You see those flats?
I live up there.
Mine's the blue window
Up in the air.

There's lifts and stairs
And doors and doors,
And twenty-seven
Identical floors.

The swings outside
Are too far away,
So we sit up here
With Mum all day.

It's good when it's cold
Up here all warm;
You can watch all the people
Out in the storm.

But if it's sunny and warm outside,
And I'm sick of TV, or I want to ride,
When Dad comes home from the early shift
He takes me down in the silver lift.

Auntie Dot

Elizabeth Honey

Auntie Dot
hasn't got a lot.
In her flat
there's a cat
a loaf of bread
a little blue bed
a rickety table
a friend called Mabel
a baked bean
a magazine
a golden fish
an ancient wish
a rug
a mug
a tin
a pin
a shell
a smell
a cup of the sea
a dead TV
and
me.

Mum, There's a Monster

Grace Knight

'There's a monster in my cupboard,
Honest, Mum, look.'
But Mum, she just ignored me,
She sat and read her book.

'He's breaking down the cupboard door,
There's splinters everywhere.
His nose is wide and snottery,
His ears are sprouting hair.

'There's a monster in the hallway,
Mum, you *must* believe me.'
But Mum said, 'Yes my darling,'
Then switched on the telly.

Great! He's eaten the coat rack,
And with it, my school jacket.
'Mum, this monster's angry,
And I think it's time to leg it!

'Mum, there's a monster,
He's right behind your chair!'
Too late for Mum to move...
Because he ate her then and there.

Marsupial Mole

Ronald Strahan

The marsupial mole
Doesn't live in a hole
Or a burrow or funnel
Or underground tunnel.
It swims through the sands
With its shovel-like hands
And the sand, as it's mined,
Simply falls in behind.
So nobody knows
How it comes or it goes
Or where it has been,
Which is why it's not seen.

Fewery, Mostery, Somery

Barbara Giles

I know a little about a lottle,
And what I don't know I keep in a bottle.

I know a much about a more,
And what I don't know I write on the door.

The tiny bit I have forgotten
I have rolled up on a reel of cotton.

If only I had learnt to count
I might have known more about a larger amount.

Arbuckle Jones

Peter Wesley-Smith

Arbuckle Jones
When flustered
Eats custard
With mustard

I'm disgustard.

Red Kangaroo

Ronald Strahan

Through mulga and malee with soft, thudding sound,
The red kangaroo moves in bound after bound
On the tips of its toes in a firm, steady pace
That covers the country with effortless grace.

Since pasture is scanty and waterholes few
In the harsh, arid home of the red kangaroo
It must travel great distances, never once stopping,
But endlessly, patiently, hopping and hopping.

The Bunyip

Oodgeroo of the Tribe Noonucal
(Kath Walker)

You keep quiet now, little fella,
You want big-big Bunyip get you?
You look out, no good this place.
You see that waterhole over there?
    He Gooborra, Silent Pool.
    Suppose it you go close up one time.
    Big fella woor, he wait there,
    Big fella Bunyip sit down there,
In Silent Pool many bones down there.
He come up when it is dark,
He belong the big dark, that one.
Don't go away from camp fire, you.
    Better you curl up in the gunya.
    Go to sleep now, little fella,
    Tonight he hungry, hear him roar,
    He frighten us, the terrible woor,
He the secret thing, he Fear.
He something we don't know.
Go to sleep now, little fella,
Curl up with the yella dingo.

Kim's Collection

David Bateson

Kim collects all kinds of things:
lolly sticks and can-top rings,
coloured straws,
jagged stones,
plastic cartons,
old white bones.
When the beach has jetsam there
Kim will fossick everywhere:
soggy seaweed,
(salty smells),
tattered feathers,
broken shells,
bits of cork and empty tins,
dry sea-urchins, fishes' fins,
chunks of charcoal
from some fire,
lengths of string

and tangled wire.
Marble pebbles, smoothed by ocean,
screw-top lids from sun-tan lotion,
half a twisting
birthday candle,
old false teeth,
a battered sandal.
Some folk scorn the weird selection
of the things in this collection;
others love
to touch and see them,
find such fun

Watching Eye

Colin Thiele

In the corner of the garden
I noticed something lie
like a little chip of glass
so I gently stooped to pry.

A tiny spider watched me
with a spider's tiny eye.

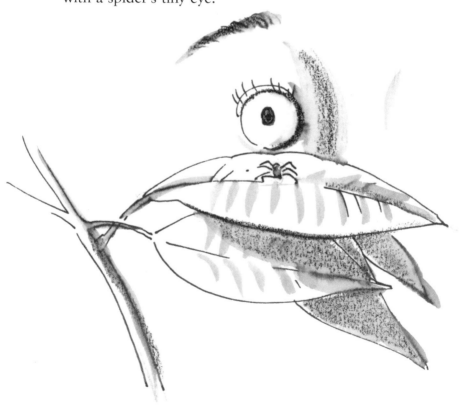

Skink

Colin Thiele

He sleeps in the sun
On the side of the hall
Like a tiny grey brooch
That is pinned to the wall;

Solitary, silent,
On his vertical bed
With his tail curved upwards,
Asleep on his head;

His skin sun-polished,
Magical, rare,
As shining and perfect
As the clear mountain air.

Then suddenly darts,
Whiplash quick —
A glint in the sunlight,
A blur on the brick.

We blink at the spot
Where his outline has lain
And search for him still...
But our search is in vain.

Hare in Summer

Flexmore Hudson

In the little strip of shade
that a strainer-post has made,
squats a weakly panting hare.
All day he has squatted there.
Only with the shade he shifts.
As I approach, he slowly lifts
his goggling eyes, but will not run,
fearing me less than the naked sun.

To Solve a Drought

Lorraine Marwood

Bird, the boy said,
Pierce the skin of the cloud above
that dark grey cloud.

Or better still, bird, unzipper
the cloud, let the inside rain
tumble out.

But if you can't pierce or unzip
try peeling it like an orange
and let the juicy rain dribble out.

I'll have my mouth open
and so will this paddock.
Bird, next year's grass seeds and insects
depend on your efforts
so fly to it
now.

The Puddle

Janeen Brian

A puddle
is a muddle
of droplets together.
A puddle
dribbles edges
in wet, rainy weather.
A puddle
can wriggle
its way to a river
to meet other puddles
with tingle and shiver.
Then, silent,
they journey
but listen to them shout,
when at the sea-mouth,
the puddles rush out!

Last Night

Anne Bell

Last night
thunder stumbled through the darkness called to the
lightning 'Bring candles.'
But the wind only blew them out again
and the rain tap-danced on the roof.

This morning
the sky is quiet, washed clean as a whistle,
only the flowers remember.

Emus

Chris Wallace-Crabbe

It is
particularly
the particular way
they come
stepping
warily
along the path
in dark
wrinkled
stockings
and shabby
mini fur coats,
their weaving
Donald Duck
heads
ready
to dip
and snatch
your ice cream
that appeals;
that,
and the way
they browse dumbly brown
in cattle-paddocks.

This Earth

Bill Neidjie

This earth...
I never damage,
I look after.
Fire is nothing,
just clean up.
When you burn,
new grass coming up.
That mean good animal soon...
might be goose, long-neck turtle, goanna, possum.
Burn him off...
new grass coming up,
new life all over.

Bwalla the Hunter

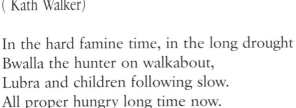

Oodgeroo of the Tribe Noonuccal
(Kath Walker)

In the hard famine time, in the long drought
Bwalla the hunter on walkabout,
Lubra and children following slow.
All proper hungry long time now.
    No more kangaroo out on the plain,
    Gone to other country where there was rain.
    Couldn't find emu, couldn't find seed,
    And the children all time cry for feed.
They saw great eagle come through the sky
To his big stick gunya in a gum near by,
Fine young wallaby carried in his feet:
He bring tucker for his kids to eat.
    Big fella eagle circled slow,
    Little fella eagles fed below
    'Gwa!' said Bwalla the hunter, 'he
    Best fella hunter, better than me.'
He dropped his boomerang. 'Now I climb,
All share tucker in the hungry time.
We got younks too, we got need —
You make fire and we all have feed.'
    Then up went Bwalla like a native cat,
    All the blackfellows climb like that.
    And when he look over big nest rim
    Those young ones all sing out at him.
They flapped and spat, they snapped and clawed,
They, plenty wild with him, my word,
They shrilled at tucker-thief big and brown,
But Bwalla took wallaby and then climbed down.

Hello Grandma

Dulcie Meddows

Hello, Grandma? Yes. It's me.
Can I speak to Granddad please?
No Mum's out shopping.
She took the baby... and Louise.
Hello, Grandma. Can I speak —
Yes I'm well. And you?
No, Dad's up on the roof,
That's why I need to speak to —
No. I'm not going to school.
Can I speak — What did you say?
No. I'm not the least bit sick.
Grandma! It's Saturday!
The antennae broke, the chimney fell
And Dad's slipped off —
Yes, Grandma! I'm listening!
What? Yes, that is a nasty cough.
Grandma, can I speak to Granddad?
Yes, of course, I still love you!
But Dad's in a predicament —
Oh all right! Kiss kiss and huggies too.
Dad's hanging off the roof, Grandma.
You remembered what?
BINGO!
No. Don't bother calling Granddad.
Yes. He goes with you... I know.
No it's Dad that's yelling Grandma.
He doesn't want to say hello.
He can't come to the phone just now.
No! You just find your purse and go.
Please hang up the phone, Grandma.
Yes. I'll tell my dad hello.
SHE'S HANGING UP THE PHONE NOW, DAD!
OKAY! OKAY! I'M RINGING TRIPLE O!

Missing Persons

Colin Thiele

The world's most enigmatic smile
Belongs to Crunch, our crocodile,
Who likes to lie in silent wait
Beside our shrubby garden gate.

And so detectives sometimes come
To question me and Dad and Mum
About the people, big and small,
Who seem to vanish when they call.

But nothing comes of it, of course,
Although we suffer some remorse,
For as they seek a sign or clue
Detectives seem to vanish too.

An Adventure Story

Furnley Maurice

There once was a man who was elephant strong,
Who trundled a rabbit-o barrow along,
Till the wind blew him on with a squeal and a whiff,
Right up to the edge of the Beaumaris cliff.
But he didn't fall over —
No! He didn't fall over —
An aeroplane passed, and he cried, 'What a boon!'
And stepped on its tail and flew up to the moon.
The pilot said 'Drop it,
Or I'll have to stop it,
I don't want to go into Heaven so soon!'

But he didn't let go it!
No! He didn't let go it!
The rabbit-o man who was elephant strong
Caught hold of a star as they hurried along;
And he said: 'I shall carry this planet with me!'
And when he got home and had finished his tea,
He hammered it into small sparking bits,
And day after day at our school-gate he sits;
And when all the children come out for their lunch.
He sells them the sparklets a penny a bunch;
And evening by evening, as everyone knows.
Richer and richer and richer he grows.

The Man From Menindee

D.H. Souter

The Man from Menindee was counting sheep;
He counted so hard that he went to sleep.

He counted by threes,
And he counted by twos.
The rams and the lambs
And the wethers and ewes.

He counted six thousand three hundred and ten,
And when he woke up he'd to count them again.

The Drovers

C.J. Dennis

Out across the spinifex, out across the sand,
Out across the saltbush to Never Never land,
That's the way the drovers go, jogging down the track —
That's the way the drovers go. But how do they come back?
Back across the saltbush from Never Never land,
Back across the spinifex, back across the sand.

Brumby Romp

Siobahn Donohoe

Galloping swiftly, coats a-glisten,
Rhythmic hoof-beats falling — listen!
Tails a-flashing, manes are tossed
Plains are covered, rivers crossed
Two horses canter stride for stride
Fiery gleam on golden hide.

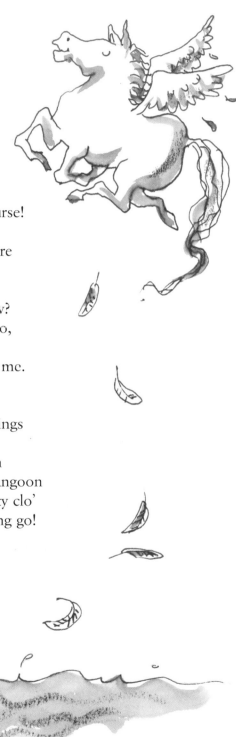

Horse

Spike Milligan

Gallop gallop gallop horse
Can you gallop? Yes of course!
Gallop gallop everywhere
Gallop here and gallop there
Can you gallop up a hill?
Gallop gallop yes I will.
Can you gallop in the snow?
Gallop yes just watch me go,
I can gallop in the sea
Splishing splashing look at me.
Can you gallop in the sky?
No but I can jump up high
If I had those feathered things
Like a pair of angel wings
I could gallop to the moon
And land in Bombay or Rangoon
So clippety cloppity clappity clo'
Grilliping golliping galloping go!

Cattle

Kelsie Loveday

Listen! Listen!
Can you hear
Something strange?
Something that goes
Moo
Clatter
Hey up
Whistle
Moo.
Do you hear?
It's, it's
Cattle,
Walking up the hill
with their new born calves.
Their sounds,
Moo Moo.
I heard a clatter!
Bang, Clatter, Boom, Moo,
It's the cattle.

Cicada

Kevin Gilbert

I'm a Cicada
I can sing
the same old thing
the same old thing
I am a Cicada
I can sing
the same old thing
the same old thing
all day.

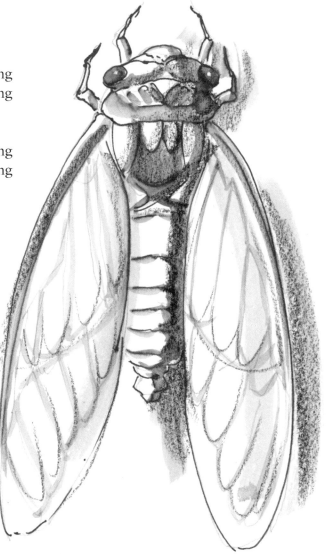

Jarrangulli

Roland Robinson
Related by Percy Mumbulla

Hear that tree-lizard singin' out,
Jarrangulli.
He's singin' out for rain.
He's in a hole up in that tree.
He wants the rain to fill that hole right up
an' cover him with rain.
That water will last him till
the drought comes on again.

It's comin' dry when he sings out,
Jarrangulli.
Soon as ever he sings out,
Jarrangulli,
he's sure to bring the rain.
That feller, he's the real rain-lizard.
He's just the same as them black cockatoos,
they're the fellers for the rain.

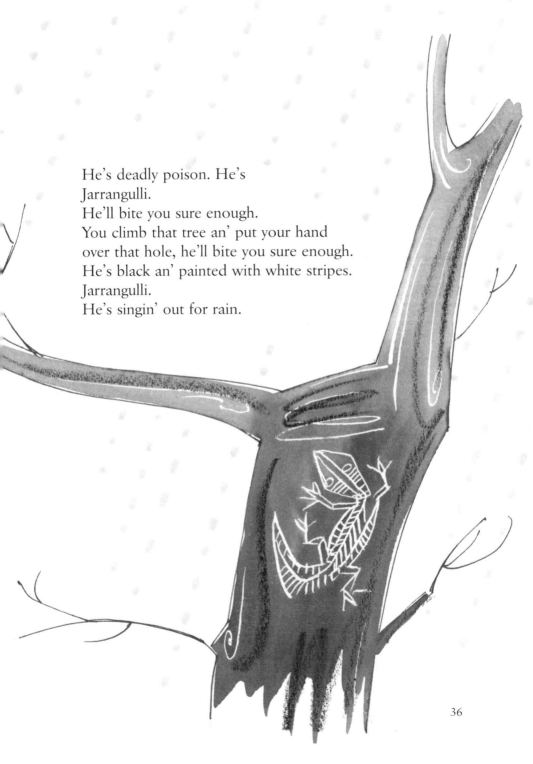

He's deadly poison. He's
Jarrangulli.
He'll bite you sure enough.
You climb that tree an' put your hand
over that hole, he'll bite you sure enough.
He's black an' painted with white stripes.
Jarrangulli.
He's singin' out for rain.

After the Rains

Irene Gough

How do they know, the wild duck flying,
How do they know there is water lying,
Lying in the claypans and the old lagoon?

Why do they leave the deep, cool River,
The tiers of rushes, where the mornings shiver
And shatter the reflections of the stars and moon?

How do they know that storms are bringing
Life to the earth, with new millions singing,
Singing in the claypans on the saltbush plains?

How do they know, the wild duck flying
The desert skyways when the winds are dying,
Ducks from the River, following the rains?

Rain, Hail, Snow

Jane Buxton

Rain drips drizzly, pitter-pat-putter
and trickles busily down the gutter.

Hail hits harshly, clitter-clat-clutter
bouncing madly in the gutter.

But snow drifts silently, soft and white,
changing everything overnight.

Seahorse

Janeen Brian

> Scales
> and a tail
>   like a question mark:
> a snout,
> and a seahorse
> bobs about.

The Rock pool

Peter Skryznecki

The rock pool
is a magic circle
full of colours the sea
washes in —
blues, greens, browns, reds:
yellow that leaps
in reflection
and does a somersault
over your head!
Seagrass weaves
in slow, soft dances —
reaches up to your face
and hands:
growing out of tiny pebbles
and the patterns
of drifting sand.
Here's a crab
that scuttles sideways,
hiding under a shelf of stone.
Look — here's a fish
with purple stripes!
And — there —
a piece of cuttlebone.
The rock pool
is a magic circle
full of treasures
from a sea king's cave —
thrown up for the delight
of children
by swirling tide
and crashing waves!

Blue-Bottles

William Hart-Smith

Someone is flying balloons
in the sea, and letting them go.
Little blue-bag balloons
with long trailing strings that sting
the white hands of earth-children.
Children of mermen and mermaids
are flying balloons
in the sea far below
and letting them go.

Sea Hunt

Evangeline Yaruso

Up again, down again,
Down to the beach again,
Go diving and diving,
Searching for seaweed.

Down again, up again,
Down to the beach again,
Go swimming and swimming,
Diving for pearls.

There and Back

Libby Hathorn

Train leaps forward
silver track
bullet fast
there and back.

I
Love the sound
murmur to scream
gnawing and gnashing
on rails that gleam.

When
Stations loom
shudder and shake,
slithers to stop
great long snake.

Then
Train leaps forward
silver track
bullet fast
there-and-back
thereandback
thereandback
there-and-back.

The Bendigo Track

Oscar Mendelsohn

Clickety clockety clack,
The Melbourne to Bendigo track,
So far as I know,
Though the train's rather slow,
It's exactly the same distance back.

Clockety clackety click,
I don't like a train that's too quick.
I prefer one that ambles,
And gambles and rambles
And stops at the shake of a stick.

Clackety clickety clock,
They've put our poor train in the dock,
The head foreman-oiler
Says 'pain in the boiler,
Its tummy is hard as a rock.'

Mulga Bill's Bicycle

A. B. ('Banjo') Paterson

'Twas Mulga Bill, from Eaglehawk, that caught the cycling craze
He turned away the good old horse that served him many days;
He dressed himself in cycling clothes, resplendent to be seen;
He hurried off to town and bought a shining new machine;
And as he wheeled it through the door, with air of lordly pride,
The grinning shop assistant said, 'Excuse me, can you ride?'

'See here, young man,' said Mulga Bill; 'from Walgett to the sea,
From Conroy's Gap to Castlereagh, there's none can ride like me
I'm good all round at everything, as everybody knows,
Although I'm not the one to talk — I *hate* a man that blows.
But riding is my special gift, my chiefest, sole delight;
Just ask a wild duck can it swim, a wildcat can it fight.
There's nothing clothed in hair or hide, or built of flesh or steel,
There's nothing walks or jumps, or runs, on axle, hoof, or wheel
But what I'll sit, while hide will hold and girths and straps are tight,
I'll ride this here two-wheeled concern right straight away at sight.'

'Twas Mulga Bill, from Eaglehawk, that sought his own abode,
That perched above the Dead Man's Creek, beside the mountain road.
He turned the cycle down the hill and mounted for the fray,
But ere he'd gone a dozen yards it bolted clean away.
It left the track, and through the trees, just like a silver streak,
It whistled down the awful slope towards the Dead Man's Creek.

It shaved a stump by half an inch, it dodged a big white-box:
The very wallaroos in fright went scrambling up the rocks,
The wombats hiding in their caves dug deeper underground,
As Mulga Bill, as white as chalk, sat tight to every bound.
It struck a stone and gave a spring that cleared a fallen tree,
It raced beside a precipice as close as close could be;
And then as Mulga Bill let out one last despairing shriek
It made a leap of twenty feet into the Dead Man's Creek.

'Twas Mulga Bill, from Eaglehawk, that slowly swam ashore;
He said, 'I've had some narrer shaves and lively rides before;
I've rode a wild bull round a yard to win a five-pound bet,
But this was the most awful ride that I've encountered yet.
I'll give that two-wheeled outlaw best; it's shaken all my nerve
To feel it whistle through the air and plunge and buck and swerve.
It's safe at rest in Dead Man's Creek, we'll leave it lying still;
A horse's back is good enough henceforth for Mulga Bill.'

My Bike

Elizabeth Honey

Dusk
wind whistles in my ears
smooth path
tyres hum
swooping through the gardens
no hands
sending the possums jumping for the trees
tailwind
I'm flying!

Free wheeling on a bike

Robert Gray

Freewheeling on a bike —
the butterflies of sunlight
all over me.

Pigeon Song

Janeen Brian

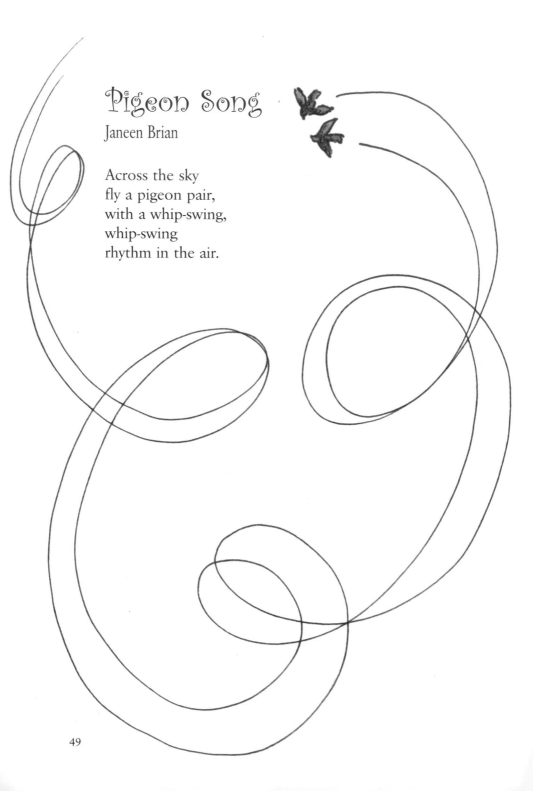

Across the sky
fly a pigeon pair,
with a whip-swing,
whip-swing
rhythm in the air.

Wind

Steven Herrick

Wind tickles the leaves of tall trees
Wind groans and complains in winter
Wind is a flag's best friend
Wind takes paper, balloons and hats for a ride
Wind and walls have fights
Wind blows up girls' dresses [don't look!]
Wind sneaks under doors
Wind is summer's air-conditioner
Wind is a bully to little yellow flowers
Wind scares men with wigs
Wind howls at the moon
Wind and sail boats are in love
Wind cries, and cries, and cries
                    then dies, until
Wind wakes, and whistles
              and shakes
              and shakes
Wind is a poem on a page
          that's here one minute
                    and
                              then
          is
blown
              away!

Catnap

Max Fatchen

My cat sleeps
with her claws
clasped
and her long tail
curled.
My cat twitches
her tabby cheek
for the mice that
squeak
and the milk that
flows
by her pink, pink nose
in the purring warmth
of my cat's world.

There Were Three Little Sheep

Mary Gilmore

There were two little sheep,
And three little sheep,
Came to see why baby
Wouldn't go to sleep.
    They peered in the window,
    And they entered at the door,
    And their hard little hoofs
    Tap-tapped on the floor.
Said the first little sheep,
'O hush-a-bye-bye!
You will wake all the lambs
In the fold if you cry!'
    And the second little sheep,
    With a shake of his head,
    Said, 'It's high time babies
    Were all away to bed.'
But the third little sheep
Never said a word,
For baby cuddled up
Like a tired little bird.
    Then the three little sheep,
    In the turning of a pin,
    Tap-tapped out
    As they tap-tapped in.
Hush-a-bye baby
Hush-a-bye-bye!
Hush-a-bye baby,
Bye-bye-bye...

Miss Strawberry's Cat and the Bouncing Rat

Eric Rolls

Once there was a bouncing rat,
Long and lean and very fat,
Lean and fat and fat and lean
Or somewhere halfway in between,
Who chased Miss Strawberry's barking cat
Round and round and round and that
So annoyed the barking cat
It humped and scrumped and clawed and spat
Which so annoyed the bouncing rat
It bared its teeth and muttered, 'Scat,'
Which so annoyed the awful cat
It caught and ate the savage rat
Which so annoyed the bouncing rat
It gnawed upon the barking cat.
Then they both began to fight
All day long then all the night
With kick and scratch and claw and bite
Until their legs were so confused
And bodies torn and so contused,
One could not see if which or what

The Drawing on the Blackboard

Elizabeth Davies

The rooster is captured
in a cage of chalk;
its bright plumage is stiff
as my dad's starched shirts.
He will have to keep his pose
until he is rubbed off the board
then, in tiny powder flakes
he flutters to the floor.

Bamboo Tiger

Michael Dugan

Bamboo grew
in the creek bed,
tall sticks
rattling in the wind.
Close, dark thickets
where tigers hid,
growling softly
as they waited to pounce.
Tiptoeing past
I would hear them,
see their round eyes
glaring from shadows.
And I would run and run,
faster than wind
across the fields.
Faster than tigers,
who returned to their thicket,
jaws slavering, outwitted again.

Coming to Get You

Libby Hathorn

One, two
I'm looking for you.
Three, four
I'll get you for sure.
Five, six
By magic tricks.
Seven, eight
And I won't wait.
Nine, ten
I'll find you, then.
Ten nine eight seven six
Five four three two
One
You'd better, you'd better,
Run Run RUN!

Who'll Buy?

Dorothy Simmons

Puppies for sale! Puppies for sale!
　Midnight yappers, sandshoe nappers,
　　Tennis-ball trouncers, wind-leaf pouncers,
　　Pocket rippers, big toe nippers,
　　　Wrigglers squigglers, snugglers cuddlers...
　　Puppies for sale! Puppies for sale!

Witches Have Hitches

John Jenkins

Witches have hitches
in their funny black britches
and bits of straw from the end of their brooms
and they often get itches
and backstroke and fitses
from flying too close to the moon.

Over the Moon

Nan Hunt

I met a cow in orbit,
I bowed and said, 'Good day.'
Next time we passed she bellowed:
'Is this the Milky Way?'

If You Go Softly

Jennifer Kelly

If you go softly out to the gum trees
At night, after the darkness falls,
If you go softly and call —
Tch, Tch, Tch
Tch, Tch, Tch,
They'll come —
the possums!
If you take bread that you've saved
They'll come close up, and stand
And eat right from your hand —
Softly,
Snatching,
Nervous —
the possums!
And if you are still, and move slowly,
You can, very softly, pat
Their thick fur, gently, like that —
It's true!
You can!
Really touch them —
the possums!
You can do that all —
If you go softly,
At night,
To the gum trees,
If you go softly
— and call.

Night Noises

Patricia Wrightson

Who's there at my window? Who's that?
Who is walking as soft as a cat
In the dark of the night?

Now it's gone — the soft paw in the grass
Or the moth-wing that happened to pass.
I have put out the light.

Cat Being Cat

Libby Hathorn

Curls in swirls
of blankets
Moulds on folds
of sheets
Sleeps on heaps
of clothing
Yowls at pals
in streets

Curls
Uncurls
Elastic
Fantastic
Cat being cat!

Waits
on gates
Tenses on fences
Climbs
on vines
Scrounges on lounges

Yawns on lawns
Naps on laps
Curls
Uncurls
Elastic
Fantastic.
How about that
Cat being cat!

I Lie Straight

Elizabeth Honey

I lie straight
eyes shut
Mum makes the bed
a soft silk breeze brushes me
as the sheet floats down
and settles on me
like a whisper

Night Noises

Christine Perkins

In the silence of the night
I can hear

an owl hooting
a cricket singing
the wind whistling
a tree creaking
a dog barking
and me breathing.

Nightening

Michael Dugan

When you wake up at night
and it's dark and frightening,
Climb out of bed
And turn on the lightening.

The Witch's Balloon

S. J. Graham

Far far away, where ganders are grey,
In a land where pixies dwell,
There once lived a witch who did nothing but stitch,
And she lived in a coconut shell.
She stitched by day and she stitched by night,
She stitched both early and soon.
For she dreamt of making a wonderful flight
In a magical gas balloon.
At last it was done. She chortled, 'What fun.'
She puffed till it grew up quite round.
Fixed a basket below, called out, 'Here we go.'
And cheered as it flew from the ground.
Inside she then hopped, and it never stopped,
High up sailed that magic balloon.
Alas and alack, she never came back...
You can see her up there on the moon!

Fall in the mall

Geoffrey McSkimming

Once a genteel alligator
   bought a coffee percolator,
      tripped up on the escalator,
         fell onto a fat ice-skater —
            both went tumbling — crashed at greater
               speed onto a dinner waiter,
                  woman with a calculator,
                     startled pest exterminator,
                        sprawling prestidigitator,
                           vacuum cleaner demonstrator,
                              schoolboy with his doting mater,
                                sailor south of the Equator,
                                runaway perambulator,
                                    out-of-work impersonator

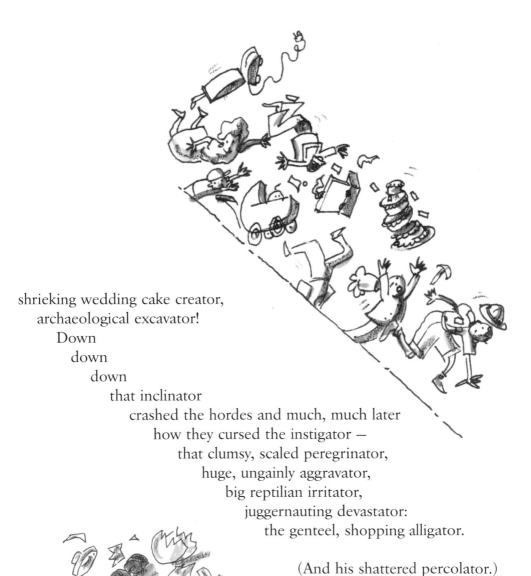

shrieking wedding cake creator,
   archaeological excavator!
      Down
         down
            down
               that inclinator
                  crashed the hordes and much, much later
                     how they cursed the instigator —
                        that clumsy, scaled peregrinator,
                           huge, ungainly aggravator,
                              big reptilian irritator,
                                 juggernauting devastator:
                                    the genteel, shopping alligator.

                              (And his shattered percolator.)

Sitting on the Fence

Michael Leunig

'Come sit down beside me',
I said to myself,
And although it doesn't make sense,
I held my own hand
As a small sign of trust
And together I sat on the fence.

Nothing

Barbara Giles

If nobody had no body
Nobody would know
No one could see anyone,
Nowhere could they go.
No one would walk up to no one
To look him in the eye,
If nobody heard no voices
No one would reply.

House On Its Own

Barbara Giles

Think of a house on its own,
everyone gone.
Nothing but air
moving from room to room,
even the mirrors are bare,
nobody there.
In the kitchen water is speaking,
if people were home they would say,
'That tap's leaking.'
Strange and lonely and not quite right,
houses need people to come home at night.

Darkling

Barbara Giles

Now it is coming,
the dark of evening,
when birds are twittering
in nightly meeting,
find eave-space for sleeping,
the sky now darkening
they cease their cheeping,
sleep overtaking,
head under wing
till morning wakening.

At Night

Raymond McCormack

When the tide comes in
and the moon
comes out,
the sea goes to bed
and all is still
as still as can be
Even the fish
sense the still
and quietly sliver
in between the rocks
and seek a place
for night.
The whole world of sea
seems to rest at night.
Even the little waves
creep silently upon
the shore.

The Pelican

Benjamin Gilmour

He sits alone,
half asleep,
with the silent waves
against his feet.
He doesn't move
his milky wings
as the salty wind
quietly sings.
He bows his head
towards the sea,
so cool and calm,
so vast and free,
The setting sun
so red and dry
slowly leaves
the scarlet sky.
But the pelican sits
upon his post,
till the break of day,
a silent ghost.

Tortoise

Anon

Long necked tortoise floats like paper bark
flying in the water.
Splash!
She dives.

The Green Frog

Colin Thiele

Because he sits there all alone
On his wet and weedy stone
While his chest heaves in and out
In a breathless sort of pout,
You would think he'd swum a race
At a fast and frantic pace
And was resting to regain
His strength and stamina again.
But actually this little king
Hasn't done a single thing
Except to sit there all the while
With a wide and gummy smile.

Giants

Lydia Pender

How would you like it –
Supposing that you were a snail,
And your eyes grew out on threads,
Gentle, and small, and frail –
If an enormous creature,
Reaching almost up to the distant skies,
Leaned down, and with his great finger touched
your eyes
Just for the fun
Of seeing you snatch them suddenly in
And cower, quivering back
Into your pitiful shell, so brittle and thin?
Would you think it was fun then?
Would you think it was fun?

And how would you like it,
Supposing you were a frog,
An emerald scrap with a pale, trembling throat
In a cool and shadowed bog,
If a tremendous monster,
Tall, tall, so that his head seemed lost in a mist,
Leaned over, and clutched you up in his great fist
Just for the joy
Of watching you jump, scramble, tumble, fall,
In graceless, shivering dread,
Back into the trampled reeds that were grown so tall?
Would you think it a joy then?
Would you think it a joy?

Going Fishing

Lexie Griffiths

When it's dull, or if the sun is gleaming
On the water, or the rain is teeming,
When the mud is splashing, or the road is dusty,
If the breeze is gentle, or the wind is gusty,
It makes no difference, for I'm always wishing —
Wishing all the time that I was going fishing.
When the hoar-frost makes the tender grass blades shiver
And twinkle on the banks beside the river,
When the bull-frogs croak, and sunsets paint the sky,
And that's the time that I am passing by,
Why, more than ever then I find I'm wishing —
Wishing all the time that I was going fishing.
It doesn't matter if it's hot or cold,
Or if the grass is green or turned to gold,
If little birds are waking in their nest,
Or if the sun is sinking in the west;
It doesn't matter, for I'm always wishing —
Wishing all the time that I was going fishing.

Windy Weather

Anne Bell

When trees are clapping their leaves together
And branches snap and grasses bend
And people say,
'Oh, isn't it dreadful weather?'
And turn their overcoats up to their chins,
I run and I jump and I shout out loud,
'I like the wind!'.
And the wind takes my words and blows them away,
Up to the clouds, with the whirling birds
And the wind-mill grass.
I think it's a wonderful day,
So it's down with my head, and up with my heels
And upside-down and inside out
The wind and I turn catherine-wheels.

Skateboard

Max Fatchen

We twist
    and we turn
        and the pavement
             we burn
                as we rocket
                downhill at a rate.
          We whoop
           and we swoop
      as we crouch
     and we stoop
        on the board
            where we ride
              when we skate.

With a shove
    and a run
        it is furious fun
            as we roll
                with a sweep
                    and a swerve.
                    Then we reel
                        and we rip
                    in a breathtaking trip
                while keeping
                    our balance
                and nerve.
            We swing
        and we sway
    in a dare-devil way
        on a hair-raising,
            zig-zagging track.
                Our father
                once tried.
                You'll find him
                    inside
                    with a very
                    large bruise
                    on his back.

My Pony

Janet Rice

One foreleg gently paws the grass,
He slithers down onto the ground,
And on his back.
His legs of black
Wave in the air,
And with great care
He lifts himself again
And my pony has just rolled.

My Mysterious Cat

Camille Irving

My cat Simba is nine.
His eyes wink at me,
like stars shining
gold at night.
Is he wishing that
he was young,
playing with his ball
or dangling in wool?
Is he thinking about
catching sardines in the park?
I wonder.

Rock, Our Dog

Nicholas Hadfield

He's dead now.
He was put to sleep last night.
I was sad,
But I did not cry.

It was not the same
Without him there
To prance and
Muzzle his head
Into my arms.

Today we were going
To bury him
In the garden.
I helped dig the hole,
And then ran off.

Old Horses

Max Fatchen

Old horses,
Leaning on fences.
Old horses,
Rubbing on trees.
Old horses,
Lazy rumps pointing
Towards the cold gusts
Of a southerly breeze.
    Old horses,
    Never a gallop.
    Old horses,
    Heavy hoofs slow.
    Old horses,
    Down by the creek-bed,
    Down on the flats
    Where the sweet grasses grow.
Old horses,
Sweeping tails twitching.
Old horses,
Tossing their manes.
Old horses,
Gone are the hauling,
The shouts of the driver,
The tug on the reins
    Old horses,
    Sleepy heads hanging.
    Old horses
    Of yesterday's teams.
    Old horses,
    Soft nostrils breathing
    The wheezy contentment
    Of hay-scented dreams.

Fifty Burly Bushrangers

Isobel Kendall Bowden

Fifty burly bushrangers
Went out to steal some gold,
But all the bush was wet with dew
And one caught a cold.
And one found a bulldog ant
Creeping in his chest,
And one had a gammsky leg
And had to have a rest.
One thought he saw a snake,
Another had a pain,
The rest, they heard a gun go off
And scampered home again.

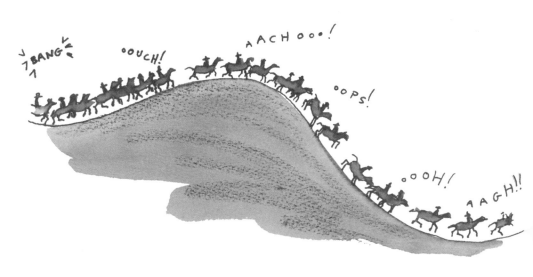

Thunderbolt

Bill Scott

Thunderbolt came from the Hawkesbury River.
He was a bushranger, he was a rover.
Made all the rich folk shudder and shiver.
Wore fine clothes and lived in clover.
Riding high on a thoroughbred colt —
Bad man, bushranger, Thunderbolt.

Uralla, Armidale, Torrington as well,
Yarrowick Mountain where the farmers dwell
saw him ride, till a constable in blue
caught him and sent him to Cockatoo;
but he slipped from his cell and his iron chain
to wander free in the bush again.

He wandered far, he wandered wide.
Nobody knows just where he died
but on Yarrowick Mountain when the wind is high
and shadowy clouds go drifting by,
riding tall on his thoroughbred colt
comes the ghost of Thunderbolt.

Comes the ghost of Thunderbolt.

The Traveller

C.J. Dennis

As I rode in to Burrumbeet,
I met a man with funny feet;
And, when I paused to ask him why
His feet were strange, he rolled his eye
And said the rain would spoil the wheat;
So I rode on to Burrumbeet.

As I rode in to Beetaloo,
I met a man whose nose was blue;
And, when I asked him how he got
A nose like that, he answered, 'What
Do bullocks mean when they say 'MooÓ?'
So I rode on to Beetaloo.

As I rode in to Ballarat,
I met a man who wore no hat;
And, when I said he might take cold,
He cried, 'The hills are quite as old
As yonder plains, but not so flat.'
So I rode on to Ballarat.

As I rode in to Gundagai,
I met a man and passed him by
Without a nod, without a word.
He turned, and said he'd never heard
Or seen a man so wise as I.
But I rode on to Gundagai.

As I rode homeward, full of doubt,
I met a stranger riding out:
A foolish man he seemed to me;
But, 'Nay, I am yourself,' said he,
'Just as you were when you rode out.'
So I rode homeward, free of doubt.

The Famine and The Feast

C. J. Dennis

Cackle and lay, cackle and lay!
How many eggs did you get to-day?
None in the manger, and none in the shed,
None in the box where the chickens are fed,
None in the tussocks and none in the tub,
And only a little one out in the scrub.
Oh, I say! Dumplings to-day!
I fear that the hens must be laying away.

Cackle and lay, cackle and lay!
How many eggs did you get today?
Two in the manger and four in the shed
Six in the box where the chickens are fed,
Two in the tussocks and ten in the tub,
And nearly two dozen right out in the scrub.
Hip, hooray! Pudding today!
I think the hens are beginning to lay.

Goosey Goosey Gander

Anon

Goosey Goosey Gander
Whither do you wander?
Your place is in the poultry yard
And not on the verandah!

Onions, Bunions...

(from *The Magic Pudding*) Norman Lindsay

'Onions, bunions, corns and crabs,
Whiskers, wheels and hansom cabs,
Beef and bottles, beer and bones,
Give him a feed and end his groans.'

Fish

Janeen Brian

Down by the sea —
there!
in the shallows,
fish, thin as silver needles,
stitching
lacy seaweed.

Rocking

Ruth Sansom

Sleep, little boy,
Your father is fishing;
Sleep, little boy,
Your mother is wishing
That father would come
With a boat full of fish
And leave us with nothing
At all to wish.
Sleep, little boy,
Your father is fishing;
Sleep, little boy,
Your mother is wishing.

Wake Up!

Tohby Riddle

Wake up stars!
It's time to rise.
You're needed now
across the skies.
You too, moon!
There's much to do.
I've done my day —
it's over to you.
Up you get!
It's my turn to sleep
and dream amidst
the heavens deep.
Just wake me
when your night is done.
And I will rise
— the morning sun.

Morning and Evening

Gwendda Mckay

I like the two ends of day,
the going out and the coming in of light,
the ending of day and the ending of night.
Each end is a beginning.
Gently the night moves back
and becomes somehow less black,
until
it's cool
and still
and morning.

> Night waits all day,
> light wants to stay,
> but at last birds noisily nest,
> the air shivers,
> the sky quivers to golden pin point
> until
> it's cool
> and still
> and evening.

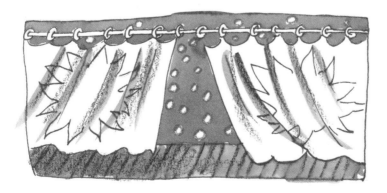

Mist

Sarah Kelly

Mist crept
while I slept
    seemed to swallow
    every hollow
grey-white over every tree
grey-cloak falling over me
    misty fingers reaching out
    misty fingers all about.
Mist crept
while I slept.

Waltz

Linda Smallman

The wind sings
With his froggy voice
And the trees
Waltz in rhythm.

On Mount Buffalo

Brian Canning

On Mount Buffalo
The trees
Are up to their knees
In snow.

Winter

Steven Herrick

yesterday
we built a big fat snowman
it was fun
but today
the snowman
          ran
                off
                    with
                          the
                                sun.

The Last Snake

William Mountford

Slippery slimy
a snake slides
with its flat head
high in the misted air.
A chill,
a cold chill slowly crinkled
up my bony spine —
its twirling scales
curling up
in the crisp morning.

Frost

Colin Thiele

Let the frost on the fenceposts
and the dew on the wire
tingle your fingertips
with icy fire.

The Rogery Birds

Mary Gilmore

I heard the wind blow over the hill,
    Bolderogery-rogery-O!
And it beat and bounced and banged with a will,
    Bolderogery-rogery-O!
But I didn't care how hard it blew,
Or if it went under the hill or through,
For I was safe and sound in the house,
Cosy and warm and snug as a mouse,
    Bolderogery! Bolderogery! Bolderogery-O!

The fire was bright, for the night was cold,
    Bolderogery-rogery-O!
The flame flew up, and the sparks were gold,
    Bolderogery-rogery-O!
But out in the marsh I heard the bleat
Of the little grey snipe, so swift and fleet,
And I heard the plover that brings the rain,
Cry out in the dark again and again,
    Bolderogery! Bolderogrery! Bolderogery-O!

Louder and louder the wind it blew,
    Bolderogery-rogery-O!
It gathered in sound as on it flew,
    Bolderogery-rogery-O!
And the Rogery-birds cried in between
The gusts that gathered so swift and keen,
While the little black children out on the plain
Cried, 'Bird of the waters bring us the rain!'
    Bolderogery! Bolderogery! Bolderogery-O!

The Donkey

Anne Bell

Her home is built of wind and sun,
Bird's song and butterfly's wings;
Roof of sky,
Carpet of grass
And the seasons hang their pictures on the wall.

Her eyes are wide and mild and kind,
Her muzzle soft as pussy-willow,
And her enormous ears hear things that we will
never know
For sometimes
She thinks she remembers a dream,
Like sounds of singing, a stable, a child
And one great, glorious star.

The Great Snake

Mary Gilmore

Into a hole into the ground he went,
Into a hole and the darkness before him;
Into the hole he went, and the dark
About him; into the hole he went
And the dark behind him.

No light of moon or sun
Was with him there;
Then with a rock earth closed him in.

Forever he sleeps, save that
Sometimes in dreams he turns.
Then the mountains are shaken.

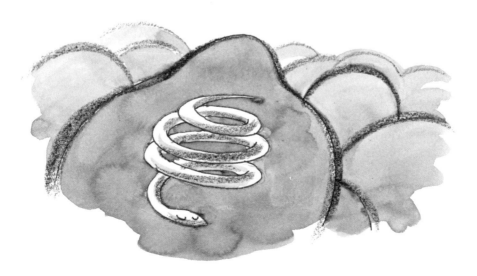

Snake

Jill McDougall

S...s...snake is very slippery,
S...s...snake is very quiet,
Silent as a sliding shadow,
S...s...snake is out tonight.

S...s...snake is coming closer,
S...s...snake is smooth as ice,
Slipping down the silvery sandhill,
S...s...snake is out tonight.

Down the sandhill, through the bushes,
Hunting frogs and hopping mice,
SNAP! She's found her slippery supper,
S...s...snake is out tonight.

Night Birds

Geoffrey Dutton

I wonder why
Birds sing by day, but at night they cry.

The curlews wail
As if they hope to find, but fail.

Oyster-catchers echo
Each other as if the beach were hollow.

The mopoke calls
How far away the darkness falls.

The rainbird spills
Notes into a dam that never fills.

Only the magpie
By moonlight sings and does not cry.

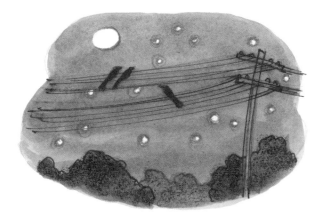

An Occasion of Parting

Elizabeth Riddell

Goodbye, the smoke said,
Blowing from the chimney,
And goodbye, the wind said,
Whistling to the bird
And the smoke and the wind
Bent to the water —
Was that goodbye he heard?
Goodbye, said the bird
To the mast raking
The clouds, and the clouds
Answered goodbye.
And the threeway talk
Went over the water,
Lost in the wind's sigh.
Goodbye, said the fish
To the wind, to the water,
I swim fast but he swims
Faster than I.
Fish, mast and bird,
Cloud, smoke and water,
Tell him we all said goodbye.

Index of Authors

MARWOOD, L. • To Solve a Drought
McCORMACK, R. • At Night
McDOUGALL, J. • Snake
McKAY, G. • Morning and Evening
McSKIMMING, G. • Fall in the Mall
MEDDOWS, D. • Hello Grandma
MENDELSOHN, O. • The Bendigo Track
MILLIGAN, S. (An honorary Australian) • Horse
MOUNTFORD, W. (10 years) • The Last Snake
MUMBULLA (Robinson) • Jarrungulli
NEIDJIE, B. • This Earth
OODGEROO (Walker) • Bwalla the Hunter • The Bunyip
PATERSON, A.B. (Banjo) • Mulga Bill's Bicycle
PENDER, L. • Giants
PERKINS, C. (11 years) • Night Noises
RICE, J. (10 years) • My Pony
RIDDELL, E. • An Occasion of Parting
RIDDLE, T. • Wake Up!
ROLLS, E. • Miss Strawberry's Cat and the Bouncing Rat
SANSOM, R. • Rocking
SCOTT, B. • Thunderbolt
SIMMONS, D. • Who'll Buy?
SKRYZNECKI, P. • The Rock Pool
SMALLMAN, L. • Waltz
SOUTER, D.H. • The Man from Menindee
STAMATIS, L. • Skediddle, Skedaddle
STRAHAN, R. • Marsupial Mole • Red Kangaroo
THIELE, C. • Frost • Missing Persons • Skink • The Green Frog
• Watching Eye
WALLACE-CRABBE, C. • Emus
WESLEY-SMITH, P. • Arbuckle Jones
WINCH, G. • Bits of Me
WRIGHTSON, P. • Night Noises
YARUSO, E. • Sea Hunt

Index of First Lines

Acknowledgements

The publishers gratefully acknowledge the following authors, publishers, literary agencies and copyright holders for permission to reproduce the numbered poems.

1: © Elizabeth Honey in *Honey Sandwich*, 1993, Allen & Unwin; **2**: © Linda Stamatis in *Big Dipper Rides Again*, 1982, Oxford University Press. Editors June Epstein, June Factor, Gwendda McKay, Dorothy Rickards; **3**: © Gordon Winch in *Mulga Bill Rides Again. A Book of Australian Poems Kids Can't Put Down*, 1988, compiled by Gordon Winch, Macmillan Australia; **4**: © Max Fatchen, and his agent John Johnson; **5**: © Jane Bradley in *Big Dipper*, 1980, Oxford University Press. Editors June Epstein, June Factor, Gwendda McKay, Dorothy Rickards; **6**: © Elizabeth Honey in *Honey Sandwich*, 1993, Allen & Unwin; **7**: © Grace Knight in *Dragon Flies, Monsters and Spies. A collection of poems by Grace Knight*, 1991, ABC Enterprises; **8**: © Ronald Strahan in *The Incomplete Book of Australian Mammals* by Ronald Strahan, 1997, Kangaroo Press; **9**: © Barbara Giles in *Up-right Downfall* compiled by B. Giles, R. Fuller, A. Rumble, Oxford University Press, Oxford.*; **10**: © Peter Wesley-Smith in *The Ombley-Gombley*, 1969 by Peter Wesley-Smith, drawings by David Fielding, Angus & Robertson; **11**: © Ronald Strahan in *The Incomplete Book of Australian Mammals* by Ronald Strahan, Kangaroo Press, 1997; **12**: © Oodgeroo from the tribe Noonucal/ Kath Walker in *The Moving Skull*, compiled by Michael Dugan, 1981, Hodder & Stoughton; **13**: © David Bateson in *Rattling in the Wind. Australian Poems for Children,* 1987, compiled by J Heylen & C Jellett, Omnibus Books, Adelaide*; **14**, **15**: © Colin Thiele in *Poems in my Luggage*, Omnibus; **16**: © Flexmore Hudson in *As Iron Hills*, Angus & Robertson; **17**: © Lorraine Marwood in *The School Magazine*, NSW Department of Education **18**: © Janeen Brian in *The School Magazine,* NSW Dept of Education; **19**: © Anne Bell in *Muster Me a Song*, Triple D Books; **20**: © Chris Wallace Crabbe in *A First Australian Poetry Book*, 1983, editor June Factor, Oxford University Press, with permission of Carcanet Press Ltd; **21**: © Bill Neidjie in *Rattling in the Wind. Australian Poems for Children*, 1987, compiled by J. Heylen & C Jellett, Omnibus Books, Adelaide*; **22**: © Oodgeroo/ Kath Walker of the tribe Noonuccal, *My People*, The Jacaranda Press, reproduced by permission of John Wiley & Sons Australia; **23**: © Dulcie Meadows in *The School Magazine* NSW Department of Education; **24**: © Colin Thiele in *Poems in my Luggage*, Omnibus; **25**: © Furnley Maurice *The Bay and Padie Book: Child Poems,* Melbourne University Press; **26**: © D.H. Souter in *One Hundred Poems Chosen for Children*, 1967 compiled by J Saxby Angus & Robertson; **27**: C J Dennis © *A Book for Kids*, 1921, Angus & Robertson; **28**: © Siobahn Donohoe in *Saddle Up Again*, editor Mary Small, Angus & Robertson, 1995, *The School Magazine*, NSW Department of Education; **29**: © Spike Milligan in *Startling Verse For All the Family*, 1987, Michael Joseph. Reproduced with permission of Spike Milligan Productions Ltd; **30**: © Kelsie Loveday in *Poems from a Wide Brown Land. The Dorothea Mackellar Memorial Poetry Competition for Schools* 1995, 1996, 1997, 1998 compiled by M Saxby & A Hoddinott, University of New England, 1998*; **31**: © Kevin Gilbert in *Child's Dreaming* with the permission of the publisher Hyland House; **32**: © Roland Robinson, related by Percy Mumbulla in *Someone is Flying Balloons*, 1983, compiled by J Heylen & C Jellett, Omnibus Books, Adelaide*; **33**: © Irene Gough, 1983, in *A First Australian Poetry Book*, editor June Factor, 1983, Oxford University Press*; **34**: © Jane Buxton in *The School Magazine*, NSW Department of Education*; **35**: © Janeen Brian in *The School Magazine,* NSW Department of Education; **36**: © Peter Skrzynecki in *Someone is Flying Balloons*, 1983, compiled by J Heylen & C Jellett, Omnibus Books, Adelaide; **37**: © William Hart-Smith. Permission from Brian Dibble, editor *Birds, Beasts, Flowers: Australian Children's Poetry by William Hart-Smith*, Ringwood, Vic. Penguin 1996; **38**: © Evangeline Yaruso in *Rattling in the Wind. Australian Poems for Children*, compiled by J Heylen & C Jellett, 1987, Omnibus Books, Adelaide*; **39**: © Libby Hathorn in *Talks with my Skateboard*, 1991, ABC; **40**: © Oscar Mendelsohn in *Stuff and Nonsense*, 1974, compiled by Michael Dugan, Collins*; **41**: © A B (Banjo) Paterson in *The Collected Verse of A B Paterson*, Angus & Robertson; **42** © Elizabeth Honey in *Mongrel Doggerel*, 1998, Allen & Unwin; **43**: © Robert Gray in *Creekwater Journal*, University of Queensland Press; **44**: © Janeen Brian in *The School Magazine,* NSW Department of Education; **45**: © Steven Herrick in *Poetry to the Rescue*, 1998, University of Queensland Press; **46**: © Max Fatchen, and his agent John Johnson; **47**. © Mary Gilmore reproduced with the permission of the publisher, ETT imprint, Sydney 2002; **48**: © Eric Rolls in *Miss Strawberry Verses*, 1978, Kestral Books*; **49**: © Elizabeth Davies in *Once Around the sun. An Anthology of Poetry by Australian Children*, compiled by B Thompson, Oxford University Press, Melbourne*; **50**: © Michael Dugan in *Rattling in the Wind. Australian Poems for Children,* compiled by J Heylen & C Jellett, 1987, Omnibus Books, Adelaide 1987; **51:** © Libby Hathorn in *Pardon my Garden*, Sally Odgers (comp) Angus & Robertson in 1992; **52:** © Dorothy Simmons in *Pardon My Garden* compiled by Sally Odgers, 1972; Angus and Robertson, Sydney; **53:** © John Jenkins in *The Moving Skull*, compiled by Michael Dugan, 1981, Hodder & Stoughton, Sydney; **54:** © Nan Hunt in *Off the Planet*, Omnibus Books, Adelaide in association with Penguin Books, 1989; **55:** © Jennifer Kelly in *Someone is Flying Balloons*, J Heylan & K Argent, Omnibus Books, Adelaide 1983*; **56:** © Patricia Wrightson in *A First Australian Poetry Book*, compiled by June Factor, Oxford University Press, Melbourne, 1983; **57:** © Libby Hathorn in *Talks with my Skateboard*, ABC, 1991; **58:** © Elizabeth Honey in *Mongrel Doggerel*, 1998, Allen & Unwin; **59:** © Christine Perkins in *Big Dipper Rides Again*, 1982, Oxford University Press. Editors June Epstein, June Factor, Gwendda McKay, Dorothy Rickards; **60:** © Michael Dugan, 1971; **61:** © S.J. Graham 1974 from *Stuff and Nonsense*, compiled by M Dugan, Collins, Sydney 1974*; **62:** © Geoffrey McSkimming, 2002. Reproduced courtesy of Curtis Brown (Aust) Pty Ltd; **63:** © Michael Leunig 1974; **64:** © Barbara Giles in *Stuff and Nonsense* compiled by M Dugan, Collins, Sydney 1974*; **65:** © Barbara Giles in *A First Australian Poetry Book*, J Factor (ed) Oxford University Press, 1983*; **66:** © Barbara Giles in *Pardon My Garden* compiled by Sally Odgers, 1992, Angus and Robertson, Sydney *; **67:** © Raymond Mc Cormack in *I Like that Stuff: Poems from Many Cultures* compiled by M Styles, 1984, Cambridge University Press, London*; **68:** © Benjamin Gilmour, 1995, in *School Magazine*, NSW Dept. of Education; **69:** Anon; **70:** © Colin Thiele in *Poems in My Luggage*, Omnibus Books/Puffin, Victoria; **71:** © Lydia Pender in *Morning Magpie*, 1984, Angus & Robertson, Sydney; **72:** © Lexie Griffiths in *Taking the Sun: Verse from Australia*, compiled by Alf Mappin, 1981, Longman Cheshire Melbourne*; **73:** © Anne Bell 2001 in *The School Magazine*, NSW Dept. of Education; **74:** © Max Fatchen, and his agent John Johnson; in *A Pocketful of Rhymes*, Max Fatchen, Puffin Books; **75:** © Janet Rice in *An Anthology of Australian Children's Poems* Oxford University Press, Melbourne*; **76:** © Camille Irving in *Poems From a Wide Brown Land* compiled by A Hoddinott and M Saxby, 1998 A.S.C. University of New England*; **77:** © Nicholas Hadfield*; **78:** Max Fatchen, and his agent John Johnson in *A Pocketful of Rhymes*, Max Fatchen, Puffin Books Melbourne*; **79:** Isobel Kendall Bowden in *Cockatoo Soup*, Jean Chapman, 1987, Hodder & Stoughton NSW *; **80:** Bill Scott in *Following the Gold*, 1989*; **81:** © C J Dennis in *A Book for Kids*, 1921 Angus and Robertson, Sydney; **82:** © C J Dennis 1921 (ibid); **83:** Anon; **84:** © Norman Lindsay in *The Magic Pudding*, 1918, Angus & Robertson, Sydney; **85:** © Janeen Brian, in *The School Magazine*, NSW Department of Education; **86:** © Ruth Samson in *A First Australian Poetry Book*, compiled by June Factor, 1983, Oxford University Press*; **87:** © Tohby Riddle, 2002. Reproduced courtesy of Curtis Brown (Aust) Pty Ltd; **88:** © Gwendda McKay from *Big Dipper Returns*, Oxford University Press, 1985; **89:** © Sarah Kelly in *Big Dipper Rides Again*, 1982, J Epstein et al Oxford University Press, Melbourne*; **90:** © Linda Smallman in *A First Australian Poetry Book*, 1983, compiled by June Factor, Oxford University Press, Melbourne; **91:** © Brian Canning in *Once Around the Sun: An Anthology of Poetry by Australian Children*, compiled by Brian Thompson, 1966, Oxford University Press, Melbourne; **92:** © Steven Herrick *Poetry to the Rescue*, 1998, University of Queensland Press; **93:** © William Mountford in *Once Around the Sun*, compiled by Brian Thompson, 1966, Oxford University Press; **94:** © Colin Thiele. First published in *Poems in my Luggage*, Omnibus; **95:** © Mary Gilmore reproduced with the permission of the publisher, ETT imprint, Sydney 2002; **96:** © Anne Bell in *Christmas Crackers: Australian Christmas Poetry*, compiled by Ann Weld, 1990, Omnibus Books, Adelaide; **97:** © Mary Gilmore, reproduced with the permission of the publisher, ETT imprint, Sydney 2002; **98:** © Jill McDougall in *Anna the Goanna and other Poems*, 2000, Aboriginal Studies Press, Canberra; **99:** © Geoffrey Dutton in *On My Island*, 1967, F W Cheshire Publications*; **100:** © Elizabeth Riddell in *Songs for all Seasons* compiled by Rosemary Dobsen, 1967, Ure Smith Sydney*.

* Every attempt was made to contact the following authors and or their agents and publishers without success.